T0400435

At the Store

LEVEL 5

/ay/ou/

Teaching Tips

Green Level 5

This book focuses on the phonemes **/ay/ou/**.

Before Reading

- Discuss the title. Ask readers what they think the book will be about. Have them briefly explain why.
- Ask readers to match the words and pictures on page 3. Read the words together.

Read the Book

- Encourage readers to break down unfamiliar words into units of sound. Then, ask them to string the sounds together to create the words.
- Urge readers to point out when the focused phonics phonemes appear in the text.

After Reading

- Encourage children to reread the book independently or with a friend.
- Ask readers to name other words with /ay/ or /ou/ phonemes. On a separate sheet of paper, have them write the words.

North American adaptations © 2024 Jump!
5357 Penn Avenue South
Minneapolis, MN 55419
www.jumplibrary.com

Decodables by Jump! are published by Jump! Library.

Library of Congress Cataloging-in-Publication Data is available at www.loc.gov or upon request from the publisher.

ISBN: 979-8-88524-745-0 (hardcover)
ISBN: 979-8-88524-746-7 (paperback)
ISBN: 979-8-88524-747-4 (ebook)

Photo Credits

Images are courtesy of Shutterstock.com. With thanks to Getty Images, Thinkstock Photo and iStockphoto. Cover – RTimages, Dragon Images, Fascinadora, monticello, Titov Nikolai, p3 –robuart, serazetdinov, Africa Studio, giedre vaitekun, Lightspring, Sudowoodo, p4–5 – mdbildes, mTaira, p6–7 – LightField Studios, VTT Studio, p8–9 – Josh Withers, Summer Photographer, p10–11 – pixfly, Rawpixel.com, Arina P Habich, p12–13 – MadamKaye, Photobac, p14–15 – New Africa, RossHelen, p16 – Shutterstock.

Can you match these words to the correct pictures?

Hay

Ouch

Runway

Sound

Mouth

Clay

There is no food on the shelf. We must delay lunch! We can get things from the store.

It is a good day to go out. Shall we go to the store?

We can pick up a basket. The food will go in the basket.

Basket

When you go around a store, you must stay near the adult you are with and do what they say.

What has this kid found next to the sprouts?
Can you say what they are called?

That is right! They are called carrots.
Can you count the number of carrots?

Perfect! There are six carrots. They will go in the basket. We will pay for them.

May we have sweets? Yes, we can!
What do you think are the best sweets?

Now we need to go pay. All the food will go on the belt. Start with the carrots and the sweets!

We must pay the person at the counter with cash. We can pay in coins.

Now we pack all the food in the bag.
We are at the end!

Look! Now the shelves are full. It was a good day at the store.

Sound out each word. Does it have an /ay/ or /ou/ sound?

cloud

mouse

spray

tray

16